Forming a Band

by A. R. Schaefer

Consultant: James Henke
Vice President of Exhibitions and Curatorial Affairs
Rock and Roll Hall of Fame and Museum
Cleveland, Ohio

Capstone
press

Mankato, Minnesota

Capstone High-Interest Books are published by Capstone Press
151 Good Counsel Drive, P.O. Box 669, Mankato, Minnesota 56002
http://www.capstone-press.com

Library of Congress Cataloging-in-Publication Data
Schaefer, A. R. (Adam Richard), 1976–
    Forming a band / by A. R. Schaefer.
    p. cm.—(Rock music library)
    Includes bibliographical references (p. 31) and index.
    Contents: Making it big—First steps—Finding band members—Band basics.
    ISBN 0-7368-2146-5 (hardcover)
    1. Rock music—Vocational guidance—Juvenile literature. [1. Rock music—
Vocational guidance. 2. Bands (Music) 3. Vocational guidance.]
I. Title. II. Series.
ML3795.S2373 2004
784.166'023—dc21   2003004519

Summary: Describes the steps musicians take to form a band, including selecting
band members, a name, music style, and appearance.

Editorial Credits
Carrie Braulick, editor; Jason Knudson; series designer; Jo Miller, photo researcher;
    Karen Risch, product planning editor

Photo Credits
Capstone Press/Gary Sundermeyer, cover, 9, 11, 12, 15, 16, 17, 18, 19, 21 (both), 25
Corbis, 5; Reuters/NewMedia Inc., 6; Neal Preston, 22, 27; S.I.N., 23

Table of Contents

Chapter 1: Making it Big   4

Chapter 2: First Steps   8

Chapter 3: Finding Band Members   14

Chapter 4: Band Basics   20

Placing an Ad   28

Glossary   30

To Learn More   31

Useful Addresses   31

Internet Sites   32

Index   32

Making it Big

The stage lights dim and the crowd begins to rumble. An explosion of light and sound blasts from the stage. The 18,000 people in the audience go wild for their favorite band. The band plays all of its hit songs. Two hours later, the band leaves the stage to more cheers from the crowd.

As they leave the arena, a group of fans buys T-shirts with the band's name on the front. On the drive home, they turn on the radio. One of the band's songs is playing. When it is over, they put in a CD of the band's greatest hits. The fans sing along with the music until they are home.

Learn about:

Concert day

Professional musicians

Famous bands

Meanwhile, the band is relaxing backstage. In the morning, they will travel to their next gig in a city miles away.

Billie Joe Armstrong of Green Day plays guitar. The band formed in the late 1980s.

Professional Musicians

The lives of professional rock musicians can be rewarding. They can make money, have thousands of fans, and travel throughout the world. But before any band becomes famous, the members make many decisions to help the band become successful. They decide who will be in the band. They also choose a style of music, songs, recording studios, and managers.

Each band forms differently. Some bands form when musicians meet at school or work. In 1970, Aerosmith formed when Steven Tyler met guitarist Joe Perry while working at an ice cream shop. Other bands form after one musician leaves a band and decides to form a new one. In 1973, Malcolm Young formed AC/DC after the band he was with broke up. Family members form some bands. Brothers Eddie and Alex Van Halen are in the band Van Halen.

CHAPTER 2

First Steps

No matter how a band forms, every band can achieve its goals easier by making good decisions. Choices that band members make at the beginning of their careers can affect their band years later.

Solo Artists and Bands

Before starting a band, musicians should know how most bands operate. Band members usually make decisions together and share money the group earns.

Some of the most popular musicians in the world are solo artists. The lead singer plays the most recognizable role in the band. Solo artists are different from bands. Solo artists normally make their own choices and keep most of the money they earn.

Learn about:

Solo artists

Band names

Trademarks

Many bands form after friends begin playing music together.

Naming a Band

Musicians who decide to start a band need to choose a name. Some bands take on the name of their lead singer, such as the Dave Matthews Band. The Eagles named themselves after a bird. Other bands get their names from day-to-day happenings. A friend of some Mötley Crüe band members said, "What a motley-looking crew," about the band.

Many bands go through several names. They often change names as they change band members or styles of music.

"... We just wanted to be the biggest thing that ever walked the planet, the greatest rock band there ever was. We just wanted everything. We wanted it all."

—Steven Tyler, lead singer of Aerosmith

Musicians can write down their ideas for band names.

Trademarks

Bands should avoid taking the names of other bands, especially if the other band is well known. Many band names have a trademark. No other band is allowed to use these names without permission. Musicians can check U.S. trademark lists to see if a name has already been used.

Bands can receive a state or federal trademark. Bands performing in one state register for a state trademark. Bands performing in more than one state register for a federal trademark.

Musicians can work together to name a band and make other decisions.

Band Names

AC/DC: One of the group's members saw "AC/DC" printed on the back of a sewing machine.

Backstreet Boys: The group played many of its first gigs in Orlando, Florida. The Backstreet Market is a shopping area in Orlando.

Ben Folds Five: The band was named for the group's lead singer, Ben Folds.

Blink-182: The band was originally called Blink, but there was already a band with that name. They then added 182.

Creed: The name came from a band that Creed member Brian Marshall was once a member of, Mattox Creed.

Phish: This band was named after the last name of the drummer, John Fishman.

R.E.M.: Lead singer Michael Stipe closed his eyes and put his finger in the dictionary. It pointed to Rapid Eye Movement, which the group shortened to R.E.M.

Veruca Salt: This band was named after a character from the book *Charlie and the Chocolate Factory* by Roald Dahl.

CHAPTER 3

Finding Band Members

One of the most important steps of forming a band is finding the right members. Band members should get along with each other and enjoy playing the same type of music.

Meeting Musicians

Musicians who want to form a band can meet other musicians in a variety of ways. Many successful bands formed after the members met each other at school.

Learn about:

Meeting musicians

Advertising for members

Auditions

Some bands form after musicians meet each other at school.

Sometimes, a choir or band teacher knows students who may be interested in joining a band. Music store workers often know about local musicians and bands. Local newspapers may have ads listing people who want to join a band.

Musicians can also post ads in newspapers or on school or music store bulletin boards. An ad should explain what qualities the musician should have, what kind of music the band plays, and contact information.

Musicians who want to form a band may check ads in local newspapers.

Teachers can help musicians find members for their band.

Handling Auditions

Musicians who are looking for others to be in a band often hold auditions. An audition can be formal or casual. A band that already has some members might invite another musician to play with them during a practice session. The band members also may have the person play solo while they listen and take notes.

Auditions can help band members decide if a musician will be right for their band.

Auditions give band members a chance to hear musicians play.

Auditions can be helpful to both the band members and the person auditioning. They give band members a chance to hear the musician. They also give the auditioner an opportunity to meet the band members and learn more about the group.

Band Basics

After forming, a band may set goals. Band members may decide to practice a certain number of days each week. They may want to book a gig in six months or decide to save money for a new piece of equipment. Musicians should write down any important goals.

Most beginning band members make their own decisions. They choose a music and clothing style. They also handle business duties for the band.

A few bands work with managers. Managers make business and creative decisions for a band. They may help a band get gigs and recording contracts. If the band makes profits, the manager receives a percentage of the money.

Learn about:

Types of rock music

Clothing styles

Practice space

Band members can make a goal to practice each week.

Music and Appearance

Bands can choose from several styles of music. Thrash, grunge, alternative, and jam are all types of rock music. In the 1990s, Nirvana and Pearl Jam became popular for their grunge music style. Today, Linkin Park and the White Stripes are popular alternative bands. Phish is one of today's popular jam bands.

Most bands start out as cover bands. These bands play songs that another band has produced. Later, groups may write their own songs.

The band Weezer plays melodic rock music and dresses in a casual style.

Bands also need to choose a style of appearance. Many rock bands wear jeans and T-shirts. Other bands have a neater appearance. Sometimes the style of music that a band plays affects its appearance. For example, thrash bands usually wear dark clothes.

Practice Space

All bands need to have space to practice. The practice area needs to be large enough to fit the band's equipment. The room also should have good acoustics. A place with good acoustics helps a band sound clear.

Band members should try to avoid bothering others when they practice. Some bands work out practice time arrangements with neighbors.

Many bands practice in garages or basements. Sometimes bands practice in soundproof rooms. These rooms keep most sound inside of them and allow little sound to enter. They usually have good acoustics.

A band's practice area should have enough space for equipment.

Working Together

Band members need to handle both musical and business matters. Some groups divide jobs between the members. One person may handle the band's money. Another person may schedule practices and keep track of goals. Some bands create fliers to promote gigs.

Good communication is important for band members. Disagreements will occur. Band members who work together to solve problems can help their band stay together.

From choosing a name to finding practice space, musicians have many decisions to make when they start a band. But the hard work is worth it as the band starts booking gigs and gaining fans.

"We have our differences, but we talk to each other. We discuss things that matter to the band with each other."

—Dave Matthews, lead singer of The Dave Matthews Band

U2

U2 is one of the most famous bands in the world. The group started in 1976 when 14-year-old Larry Mullen Jr. posted a notice at school in Dublin, Ireland. Mullen was a drummer. The notice said that he was looking for other people to be in a band. He held an audition in his kitchen. Mullen asked four people to join the band. They were Adam Clayton, Dave Evans, now known as The Edge, Dik Evans, and Paul Hewson, who became known as Bono. They called the band Feedback. The members soon changed their name to The Hype. In 1978, Dik Evans left the band, and its name became U2.

During the next couple of years, U2 played many local gigs. The band gained fans. In 1980, U2 signed a recording contract with Island Records. Since then, the group has sold millions of CDs and performed in concerts throughout the world. In 2002, U2 won four Grammy awards.

Placing an Ad

Placing an ad in a newspaper, on a music store bulletin board, or on an Internet site can be a helpful way to find band members. You can use this checklist to make an ad that will help you get quick results.

✓ Name of your band

✓ Type of musician you want (bass, lead guitar, drums, etc.)

✓ Personal qualities or skills the musician should have

✓ Type of music your band plays

✓ How many times a week the group will practice

✓ Goals of your band (For example, mention if your band expects to perform local gigs in six months.)

✓ Contact information with name and phone number

Starting a Band

Radio Slave, a local hard rock band, is looking for two talented musicians to play lead guitar and drums. Previous band experience a plus but not necessary. Must be prepared to practice at least twice a week and be available to play gigs on weekends starting this fall. Please contact Brian for an audition at the following phone number or e-mail address:

(555) 555-1234
band@radioslave.com

Glossary

acoustics (uh-KOO-stiks)—the way a room reflects sound; rooms with good acoustics allow people to hear music clearly.

audition (aw-DISH-uhn)—a short performance by a musician to see whether he or she will be right for a band

flier (FLY-ur)—a printed piece of paper that tells about an upcoming event

gig (GIG)—a live performance in front of an audience

manager (MAN-uh-jur)—a person who takes care of the business duties of a band; managers help bands get gigs and recording contracts.

solo artist (SOH-loh AR-tist)—a musician who is the star performer of a band; solo artists usually perform alone or with backup musicians.

soundproof room (SOUND-proof ROOM)—a room that lets very little sound in or out of it

trademark (TRADE-mark)—a word, picture, or design that can only be used by the owner; trademarks usually are registered with the government.

To Learn More

Anjou, Erik. *Aerosmith.* Galaxy of Superstars. Philadelphia: Chelsea House, 2002.

Morgan, Sally, and Pauline Lalor. *Music.* Behind Media. Chicago: Heinemann Library, 2001.

Rosenthal, Michèle. *Rock Rules!: The Ultimate Rock Band Book.* New York: Scholastic, 2000.

Useful Addresses

Rock and Roll Hall of Fame and Museum
One Key Plaza
Cleveland, OH 44114

RockWalk
7425 Sunset Boulevard
Hollywood, CA 90046

Rolling Stone Magazine
1290 Avenue of the Americas
New York, NY 10104-0298

Internet Sites

Do you want to find out more about rock bands?
Let FactHound, our fact-finding hound dog, do the research for you.

Here's how:

1) Visit *http://www.facthound.com*
2) Type in the **Book ID** number: **0736821465**
3) Click on **FETCH IT**.

**FactHound will fetch Internet sites picked by our editors
just for you!**

Index

acoustics, 24
ads, 16, 28–29
audition, 18–19, 27, 29

clothing, 20, 23
communication, 26
cover bands, 22

gigs, 5, 20, 26, 27, 28, 29

money, 7, 8, 20, 26
music style, 7, 10, 14, 20, 22, 23

name, 4, 10, 12, 13, 26

solo artist, 8
soundproof rooms, 24

trademark, 12